World Black History

Making Their Mark

Spring Hermann

www.raintreepublishers.co.uk
Visit our website to find out
more information about
Raintree books.

To order:

☎ Phone 0845 6044371

📄 Fax +44 (0) 1865 312263

💻 Email myorders@raintreepublishers.co.uk

Customers from outside the UK please telephone +44 1865 312262

Raintree is an imprint of Capstone Global Library Limited, a company incorporated in England and Wales having its registered office at 7 Pilgrim Street, London, EC4V 6LB – Registered company number: 6695582

Text © Capstone Global Library Limited 2010
First published in paperback in 2011
The moral rights of the proprietor have been asserted.

Edited by David Andrews, Louise Galpine, and Abby Colich
Designed by Ryan Frieson and Betsy Wernert
Illustrated by Mapping Specialists
Picture research by Mica Brancic
Originated by Heinemann Library
Printed in China by China Translation and Printing Services, Ltd.

ISBN 978 0 431194 04 2 (hardback)
14 13 12 11 10
10 9 8 7 6 5 4 3 2 1

ISBN 978 0 431194 11 0 (paperback)
15 14 13 12 11 10
10 9 8 7 6 5 4 3 2 1

British Library Cataloguing in Publication Data
Hermann, Spring
Making their mark. – (World black history)
909'.0496-dc22
A full catalogue record for this book is available from the British Library.

Acknowledgements

We would like to thank the following for permission to reproduce photographs: ©Alamy pp. **12** (North Wind Picture Archives), **34** (North Wind Picture Archives); ©ARS, NY and DACS, London 2009 pp. **20** (©2008, Digital Image, The Museum of Modern Art, New York/Scala, Florence), **42** (©2004 Foto Smithsonian American Art Museum/Art Resource/Scala, Florence); ©The Art Archive p. **19** (Museu Nacional de Belas Artes Rio de Janeiro Brazil/Dagli Orti); ©The Bridgeman Art Library pp. **10** (Private Collection), **11**, **17** (Royal Geographical Society/Harry Hamilton Johnston), **21** (Giraudon); ©Corbis pp. **4** (Bettmann), **13** (Bettmann), **26** (Bettmann), **30** (Underwood & Underwood), **33** (Bettmann), **39** (John Springer Collection) **43** (Bettmann); ©Getty Images pp. **5** (Fox Photos), **6** (MPI), **7** (Hulton Archive/O. Pierre Havens), **8** (The Bridgeman Art Library/Private Collection), **23** (Hulton Archive/Stringer), **27** (Popperfoto), **29** (Popperfoto/Rolls Press), **31** (Hulton Archive), **36** (Michael Ochs Archives), **37** (Hulton Archive), **40** (Popperfoto/Bob Thomas), **41** (Popperfoto); ©Imperial War Museum p. **25** (Ministry of Information First World War Official Collection); ©National Army Museum p. **15** (National Army Museum); ©Redferns p. **35** (Deltahaze Corporation); ©TopFoto p. **38** (The Granger Collection); ©University of Massachusetts pp. **22** (Special Collections & University Archives W.E.B. Du Bois Library), **28** (Special Collections & University Archives W.E.B. Du Bois Library).

Cover photograph of Duke Ellington and Ivie Anderson reproduced with permission of Getty Images/© Michael Ochs Archives.

We would like to thank Marika Sherwood and Stephanie Davenport for their invaluable help in the preparation of this book.

Contents

Some words are shown in bold, **like this**. You can find out what they mean by looking in the Glossary.

New beginnings after slavery

In the 1800s, slavery finally ended in many countries. In Great Britain, the Caribbean islands, the United States, South America, India, and most of Africa, slavery was illegal. In the United States, it took a bloody Civil War to free the millions of enslaved people. Most other countries ended the practice peacefully. A new time of freedom was beginning for black people around the world.

A search for a new life

Those former slaves who began new lives of freedom did not have an easy path. Opportunities varied in each nation, and governments usually offered little aid. Many freed blacks lived on farms and **plantations** for little pay. They had to keep working for their former masters, since they had no social support to help them leave.

A black family enjoys the freedom of living in their own house in the 1890s.

Freed Virginia slave Charles Crawley had to sneak his family onto empty boxcars on a train to get away from their former owner. The Crawleys found low-paying jobs until they pooled their money to buy a little land from an African-American woman. Finally, they bought a home in Petersburg, Virginia, of which Crawley proudly said they "laboured and worked for with the sweat of our brow and with these hands".

Where was equality?

Even in nations where slavery was now outlawed, fear, ignorance, and **prejudice** kept whites from trusting blacks. Black people did not have equal rights under the law to help them get jobs and housing. In many nations, blacks could not use public facilities or go to school. Despite these obstacles, blacks moved ahead with their lives. By the 1930s, many had become great scholars, leaders, artists, and athletes. Although **discrimination** made it difficult, black people around the world were making their mark.

Olympic athlete Jesse Owens became a symbol of black success.

Freedom is just a word

When slavery was outlawed, blacks were "free". But they did not have the same rights as other citizens. Whites still controlled society in many ways. Whites created the laws that discriminated against blacks. Around the world, true freedom was not yet a reality.

Legal changes

After the Civil War, the United States **Constitution** was amended to give four million African Americans their freedom. The 13th, 14th, and 15th **Amendments** promised freedom and citizenship to African Americans and gave the right to vote to African-American men.

These new laws changed life in many ways for African Americans. They could now marry and raise families without worrying that they would be sold off and split apart. New churches for blacks were built. Black men could vote, sit on juries, and even run for office. Two African Americans from Mississippi were elected to the United States **Senate**: Hiram Revels in 1870 and Blanche K. Bruce in 1875.

These politicians are celebrating the passage of the 13th Amendment in 1865. The 13th Amendment ended slavery.

Sharecropping: one step from slavery

For many African Americans, however, a life of "freedom" did not mean major changes. Freed African Americans had no land to work, few skills, and little money. Many had no choice but to work for their former masters, who needed labourers for their land.

A new system called **sharecropping** was developed. In this system, freed African Americans rented land to farm from whites. The entire crop had to be handed over to the owner for sale, from which the sharecroppers got a small share of the profit. Sharecroppers had to buy their supplies from a white-owned store. Since most freed African Americans could not read or do mental arithmetic, they were often cheated.

African-American sharecroppers work hard picking cotton in the 1890s.

The Freedmen's Bureau

In 1866 the United States government created the Freedmen's Bureau to help freed African Americans. Congress, the national law-making body, gave the Bureau funds to provide food, give medical care, and build schools. They also oversaw labour contracts that workers such as sharecroppers had to sign. The Bureau tried to make sure the workers were given some protection.

New schools

Educational opportunities for African Americans spread throughout the United States as the Freedmen's Bureau built and staffed 1,000 schools. A few schools for African-American students had existed in the North, but there were none in the slaveholding states. From 1866–70, about 150,000 African-American children received free education. The United States Congress closed the Freedmen's Bureau in 1870 because of lack of funding. Although 21 per cent of freed slaves could read and write, black schools received little government support.

Education in the British colonies

In the British **colonies** in the Caribbean, such as Jamaica, education for blacks began even before the end of slavery in 1838. Three groups of missionaries ran Jamaica's schools. The children were taught the same common subjects as whites. However, as in many countries around the world, black and white children were taught in separate schools. This practice would continue for a century.

This building in New Orleans, USA became the Abraham Lincoln School for Freedmen in 1866.

African Americans wanted more than primary education. So they worked to create their own universities. Many African-American universities were founded at this time, mainly by church organizations. In 1881 former slave Booker T. Washington founded the Tuskegee Institute, a college that trained African Americans to become teachers and work in other skilled professions.

Black Codes

When slavery ended, new laws were put in place to restrict the lives of freed blacks. These laws, called "**Black Codes**", sometimes made it seem as though slavery hadn't really ended. Restrictions in some 1865 Codes said that African Americans had to get permission from their "master" to leave the property and had to help their "master" defend his property. No African American could become an artisan, mechanic, or shopkeeper unless he bought a licence from a judge. Licences cost $100 (around £1,000 in today's money), more money than almost any former slave had.

The codes were revised in 1866, but the new ones still restricted the lives of African Americans. There were also unwritten "codes" that whites followed, such as not renting or selling homes to blacks. This kept African Americans working on plantations.

No blacks allowed

In 1900 the following facilities were segregated around the United States:

- Many schools in many cities
- Trains, buses, and trams
- Railway stations and waiting rooms
- Hotels, restaurants, taverns, and cafes
- Public playgrounds and swimming pools
- Theatres
- Telephone booths
- Cemeteries
- Hospitals

Dan Rice, a white actor in black make-up, plays Jim Crow in an American stage play in 1930.

Jim Crow laws

Along with Black Codes, local governments passed laws to make sure blacks remained "second-class citizens". These laws were intended to separate white citizens from black citizens.

"**Jim Crow**" became the common term for laws that kept African Americans **segregated**. In stage shows at that time, the character "Jim Crow" was a white actor who blackened his face and did a mocking imitation of African Americans. He performed silly dances and sang songs. The "Jim Crow" laws showed how whites looked down on African Americans. Service areas, transport, hotels, and restaurants in many parts of the country restricted African Americans to certain sections. Schools were also segregated. Areas for blacks were in worse condition than the white areas.

Legal challenges

To combat this unequal treatment, Congress passed the 1875 Civil Rights Act. It said that all Americans were entitled to the same treatment, regardless of race. Everyone could use public transport and facilities. The Act was enforced until 1883, when the **Supreme Court** ruled against the Act. Segregation returned.

Taking Jim Crow to court

In 1892 Homer Plessy decided to test the Jim Crow laws in his state of Louisiana. The laws said he could not travel in a first class train carriage. Blacks had to sit in the lower class "smoker" carriages. When he was arrested for breaking this law, he sued the railway company. His case, called *Plessy v. Ferguson*, was argued before the Supreme Court in 1896.

"Separate but equal"

Only one person voted in Plessy's favour. Justice John Marshall Harlan said the United States Constitution should be "colourblind", meaning that citizens should be treated equally, regardless of race. The other justices said the railway had the right to decide who travelled in first class carriages.

This ruling affirmed the idea that African Americans and whites could be kept "separate but equal". As long as African Americans were provided an "equal" service in education, transport, or public facilities, they could be kept separate from whites. Unfortunately, the services and facilities available to African Americans were almost always far from equal.

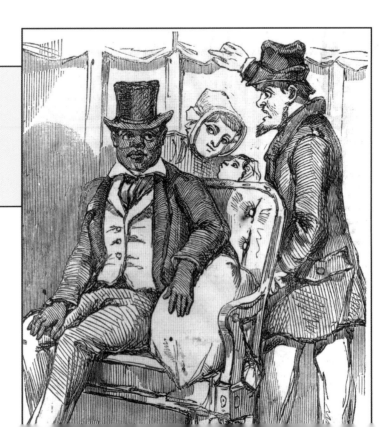

This black passenger is being asked to leave a railway carriage in Philadelphia, USA in 1856.

The Ku Klux Klan

The **Ku Klux Klan** (KKK) was a club of veterans from the Civil War who had fought on the side of the South. It was formed in 1866. After the South lost the Civil War, these veterans were angered by the freedom granted to African Americans. At first, they accosted African Americans while wearing white sheets and acting like "ghosts" to scare them. Soon the KKK's nighttime ghostly rides turned violent. They beat or killed blacks, burned their property, and took revenge on any whites who were helping blacks. They tried to influence elected officials, sometimes by bribery, sometimes with threats.

The KKK was shut down after laws limited their activity in 1870, but was formed again in 1915. It recruited members using theories about black people being inferior to whites. They began intimidating Catholics and Jews as well as African Americans. By 1921 the KKK claimed to have 100,000 members throughout the central and southern United States. They burned crosses on the property of African Americans. They paraded regularly through city streets, shouting hateful slogans.

This 1871 illustration shows members of the Ku Klux Klan surrounding a man who begs for his life.

This drawing shows a black man hanged and shot, then his body burned, in an 1863 lynching in New York City.

Lynching

From 1880 to 1930, over 5,000 African Americans were victims of racist violence in the United States. Many were **lynched** (illegally executed) by racist mobs.

Most victims were killed by hanging, while others were shot, beaten to death, drowned, or burned alive. Hundreds of European **immigrants** were also lynched. In some cases, African-American victims were in prison, awaiting trial for a crime. Mobs broke in, took these people, and executed them. Most lynchings were done in public. Crowds came a long way to watch and even celebrate the murders.

Ida Wells-Barnett

African-American journalist Ida Wells-Barnett spoke out against lynchings. In 1892 three successful African-American shopkeepers were attacked by jealous whites in Memphis, Tennessee. When the shopkeepers fought back, they were arrested and lynched.

Wells-Barnett wrote in her paper, *Free Speech*, that this lynching showed that "neither character nor standing avails the Negro if he dares to protect himself against the white man". Memphis citizens destroyed Wells-Barnett's newspaper office, so she moved to Chicago. She kept working for a national anti-lynching law and for African-American rights.

Fighting oppression globally

By the late 1800s, the enslaved blacks in most European **colonies** in Africa and the Caribbean were free. Yet it was hard for them to move forward. They were still denied equal rights. European governments took control of their lands and mines, and restricted their lives.

African colonies established

Beginning in the mid-1800s, the European nations of Great Britain, the Netherlands, France, Germany, Spain, Belgium, and Portugal all established colonies in Africa. Many fought over these areas. To settle property rights, the Berlin Conference was held in Berlin, Germany, in 1884 and 1885.

The Conference defined which nations had the right to control an area. Fourteen countries participated, but not the United States nor any from Africa. The native residents of Africa and their traditional boundaries and cultures were not considered.

EUROPE

ATLANTIC OCEAN

MADEIRA (PORT.)
IFNI
CANARY IS. (SP.)
RIO DE ORO

SPANISH MOROCCO
MOROCCO
TUNISIA
Mediterranean Sea

ASIA

ALGERIA
LIBYA
EGYPT

Red Sea

GAMBIA
FRENCH WEST AFRICA
ANGLO-EGYPTIAN SUDAN
ERITREA
SOMALILAND

PORT. GUINEA
SIERRA LEONE
LIBERIA
GOLD COAST
TOGOLAND
NIGERIA
CAMEROON
FRENCH EQUATORIAL AFRICA
ABYSSINIA (ETHIOPIA)

SÃO TOMÉ & PRÍNCIPE (PORT.)
RÍO MUNI
UGANDA
KENYA

BELGIAN CONGO
GERMAN EAST AFRICA (TANGANYIKA)
SEYCHELLES (G.B.)
ZANZIBAR (G.B.)

CABINDA
NYASALAND
COMORO IS. (FR.)

ANGOLA
NORTHERN RHODESIA
GERMAN SOUTHWEST AFRICA (NAMIBIA)
SOUTHERN RHODESIA
MOZAMBIQUE
MADAGASCAR

WALVIS BAY (G.B.)
BECHUANA LAND
SWAZILAND
SOUTH AFRICA
BASUTOLAND

Nations claiming colonies
- Belgium
- Britain
- France
- Germany
- Italy
- Portugal
- Spain
- Independent

0   500   1000 miles
0   500   1000 kilometres

N W E S

INDIAN OCEAN

This map shows the boundaries decided at the Berlin Conference in 1884 and 1885.

Fighting British Rule

In South Africa, European forces fought against native tribes, such as the Zulu nation. The Zulus had a well-trained army, and by 1879 they had beaten British forces. But the British sent more soldiers. Finally, the Zulu nation was crushed. After this, whites ran South Africa. The large black majority was kept under harsh control.

Nigeria

Nigeria became a British **Protectorate** in 1900. It was split in half by the Niger River. Some **Western** educational and economic systems were developed in the southern province. Traditional ways of living remained strong in the northern province. This division kept native groups from uniting to fight for independence from the British.

This painting shows a battle between the British and the Zulu nation in South Africa.

French colonies

In French colonies, governors tried to impose their own culture and law on the people. Like most colonial powers, they wanted large profits. French governors used forced labour and imprisonment to make the natives work harder for them. They wanted the Africans to think of themselves as French men and women but without the same rights.

Afro-Cubans seek equality

For centuries Cubans depended on slave labour to run their sugar **plantations** and rum **distilleries**. Cuban owners fought to keep their black (Afro-Cuban) slaves, but with the passage of the **Emancipation** Act in 1880, slavery ended without a civil war. All slavery was phased out by 1888.

Still under the rule of Spain, freed Afro-Cuban workers had to find jobs and places to live. Deciding they would do better in a free nation, most Afro-Cubans fought alongside whites to gain independence. Spain granted Cuba its independence in 1898.

However, a culture of *el racismo* (racism) remained strong. Afro-Cubans did not get the rights they fought for, so they formed their own Colored Independence Party in 1908. When President José Gómez tried to destroy this party, a race war broke out. Many Afro-Cubans were imprisoned or killed by government forces in the "Little War of 1912".

The Little War of 1912

In 1912 the Cuban Army killed thousands of Afro-Cubans in what became known as the "Little War of 1912". The conflict began after the Colored Independence Party was formed to give a voice to Afro-Cubans.

Fearing that their power would be reduced, Cuban leaders outlawed race-based political parties. The Colored Independence Party was criticized in the media, and members held protests across the island. Party leaders, fearing for the protesters' safety, requested weapons from the American owners of sugar mills. Instead, the United States government sent marines to protect American-owned property.

Soon the Cuban Army attacked the demonstrators, and more than 6,000 people were killed. The Colored Independence Party was all but destroyed.

This photograph shows Caribbean workers in the early 1900s.

Caribbean residents move on

The islands of the Caribbean had been colonised by several nations. The British ruled 17 island colonies. A British governor ruled each one according to British law. The Dutch controlled five islands. The French retained two main islands and nearby smaller islands, and split St. Martin with the Dutch. Spain controlled three islands. With so many languages and cultures, Caribbean residents of African descent were not able to develop a common identity.

Most black Caribbean children did get to go to primary school. However, good jobs for black adults were scarce. Many families decided to move to Britain or the United States. They hoped for better jobs and less **discrimination**. By 1924 over 12,000 Caribbean residents had moved to the United States. Most could speak English, and 70 per cent were educated professionals or skilled workers. Caribbean people had built better lives for themselves.

South American and Mexican Blacks

Blacks in South America and Mexico were enslaved for centuries. They had to struggle long and hard for freedom and equal rights. Many have still not achieved equal rights, but they have made their mark on local culture. Here are a few of their stories.

Mexico

During the slave trade, many Mexican cities were ports of entry for enslaved Africans. Many African slaves became the property of Mexicans. The country was also a haven for escaped slaves from the United States. Mexico's second president, Vicente Guerrero, abolished slavery, and all slaves were freed by 1829. But laws restricted freed blacks. They could not dress like Spaniards unless married to one, and they could not gather in groups. Craftspeople could not join guilds (unions). Most blacks could only get jobs as labourers and domestic workers. However, **intermarriage** between Spanish, native, and black persons became common. By 1900 many blacks were of mixed race. They were no longer considered African.

Argentina

Africans were enslaved in Argentina until 1853. The Spanish government was more interested in defeating the native tribes than restricting the blacks. The government also encouraged white Europeans to settle in Argentina. Most freed blacks left the farms and moved to the cities. They got jobs and intermarried with whites and natives. Only a few thousand Afro-Argentines remained.

Peru

Peru freed its black slaves during an 1854 civil war. Most had been working on plantations and in mines. As blacks migrated to large cities, owners replaced them with **indentured** Chinese workers. By 1875 more Asians lived in Peru than Afro-Peruvians. Since blacks were discriminated against, they encouraged their children to marry people of other races. However, African influence in their culture, music, and sports was strong.

This painting from 1892 shows black Brazilians working on a plantation.

Brazil

This nation had the largest population of African descent in the Americas. Brazil became the last Western nation to outlaw slavery in 1888. Many freed black Brazilians relocated to Africa, while others continued working on plantations where they had been forced to work as slaves. Equal rights laws were passed in Brazil, but blacks suffered from oppression and racism. Bias against them kept them in poor slums called *favelas*, and they earned far less money than whites.

In search of a better life

By the end of the 1800s, blacks made up 12 per cent of the United States population. Of those, 89 per cent lived in the Southern states, mostly **sharecropping** on farms. In 1913 cotton prices crashed. Then boll weevils (a pest that eats cotton) and floods ruined crops. Many African-American farmers decided to leave the countryside to try life in a big city.

The great migration

Between 1910 and 1930, many African Americans in the South learned of opportunities in the North. With some employees away fighting overseas in World War I, some northern companies sent agents south to recruit African-American workers. Black newspapers advertised new jobs in factories and shops. Taking what little they had, more than one million African Americans deserted the **plantations** of the South and boarded trains and **migrated** to cities farther north. Detroit, Cleveland, New York, Chicago, Newark, and other northern cities saw huge increases in African-American residents.

In his painting, *The Great Migration*, Jacob Lawrence, shows blacks leaving the southern United States to find work in the northern cities.

Racial conflicts explode

As African Americans found work in the cities and began voting in larger numbers, some whites grew resentful. In the southern city of Atlanta, Georgia, where many African Americans had gone in search of jobs, **riots** broke out. During the elections of 1906, Atlanta politicians stirred racial tensions by reporting alleged assaults on four white women by African-American men. This incident was never proven, but the accusations led to a race riot. Over 10,000 whites beat African Americans and looted their homes. Dozens were killed. After this, African Americans lived close together in their communities for protection.

In Springfield, USA, in July 1908, another riot broke out when an African-American man was accused of breaking into a white man's home and later killing him. Two thousand African Americans ran from the city, and many never returned. Dozens of homes and businesses belonging to African Americans were ruined. Innocent men were murdered while defending their property. The National Guard finally restored order. These riots showed how unhappy many whites were to have African Americans living beside them as equals.

This illustration shows race riots in the streets of Atlanta, USA.

The NAACP fights for justice

This photograph shows members of the NAACP after a meeting in 1929.

The 1909 founding of the National Association for the Advancement of Colored People (NAACP) in New York was a step forward in the fight for equal rights for African Americans. Several white leaders joined African Americans Ida Wells-Barnett and W. E. B. Du Bois in founding the organization. They wanted civil and political justice for all. The group grew and even opened an office in Britain.

The NAACP launched many national protests. One accused President Woodrow Wilson of keeping African-American employees **segregated** in Federal Government offices. Another protested against *The Birth of a Nation*, a 1915 film that idealised the **Ku Klux Klan** and portrayed African Americans as evil.

The NAACP sued for justice in the courts. One famous victory came in 1923. The **Supreme Court** ruled that African Americans had the right to serve on juries in every state. This made it more likely that African Americans would have fair trials in court.

W. E. B. Du Bois

NAACP cofounder W. E. B. Du Bois (1868–1963) was a scholar, speaker, author, and newspaper editor. He was the first African American to earn a Ph.D. from Harvard University. He wrote great works of African-American politics, history, and literature, including the classic *The Souls of Black Folk*.

As Publications Director for the NAACP, Du Bois edited their journal *Crisis*. In 1906 he wrote, "We want full **manhood suffrage** and we want it now. We want **discrimination** in public accommodations to cease ... we want the Constitution of the country enforced!" He wrote in a **militant** way, but believed in ending discrimination lawfully, without violence.

In 1900 Du Bois attended the first Pan-African conference, a meeting of people of African heritage from around the world (see page 28). Its goal was to rally Africans everywhere to work together to solve the problems the continent faced. Du Bois went on to organize several conferences himself, and worked the rest of his life for the cause of African unity. He saw his goal realised in 1963, when the Organization of African Unity was formed. Three months later, he died in Ghana at age 95.

Conflict at home, war abroad

Between 1916 and 1926 blacks took part in a world war, in resistance to colonial powers, and in fights in the cities of Britain and the United States. Blacks fought these battles to achieve freedom for the world and their homelands, and equality for themselves.

Blacks enlist in World War I

In 1914 the assassination of Austrian leader Archduke Franz Ferdinand led to war between nations around the world. The Allied Powers, including France, Great Britain, and Russia, went to battle with the Central Powers, which included Germany, the Austro-Hungarian Empire, and the Ottoman Empire. The United States, which entered the war in 1917, joined forces with the Allied Powers.

Over 400,000 black soldiers were enlisted in the United States Army. About 350,000 were sent to Europe. Most were members of African-American units, but not armed for combat. Their jobs included preparing food, managing supplies, driving vehicles, and digging trenches. Many wanted to go into battle, but since the United States military was **segregated**, they were not trained for combat and not sent to fight with European soldiers until later.

This map shows the Central Powers, the Allied Powers, and the nations that stayed neutral in World War I. The United States joined the Allied Powers in 1917.

Black soldiers from around the world joined the fight in World War I. Black British soldiers such as Walter Tull (see page 40) served with distinction, despite facing racism. The British West Indies regiment, a group of Caribbean soldiers who volunteered to fight with the British, served in France, Africa, and other areas, earning many medals despite limited service time. For the United States, a black division from New York fought alongside the French armed forces. They became the first allied unit to reach the border of Germany. All 171 members of the division received medals for their bravery.

The British West Indies regiment fought for Britain during World War I.

Equal regard for all

British and French troops, although mainly white, had no problem fighting alongside African Americans. France awarded the Croix de Guerre – their medal of honour – to many blacks. It is estimated that over 350,000 African-American men served and 5,180 died on the battlefields of France. The experience of "equal regard" impressed African-American soldiers. Yet when they came home to the United States, **discrimination** awaited them.

Violence continues

During and after World War I, African Americans continued to seek jobs in urban areas. Competition for jobs and housing led to more racial conflict. Any incident could set off a fight, and police were often unable to stop the violence.

On 2 July 1917, violence broke out in the city of East St. Louis, Illinois. Journalist Ida Wells-Barnett interviewed 50 eyewitnesses. Their horror stories of brutal beatings, burnings, and slayings of African Americans by white men, women, and boys showed an explosion of hatred. Wells-Barnett said that although the Illinois **National Guard** arrived to try to stop the violence, they were "**indifferent** or inactive". Hundreds of African Americans were killed or severely wounded. Although they tried to defend themselves, over 6,000 lost their homes and businesses.

Over the next four years, race **rioting** occurred in Houston, Philadelphia, Chicago, and many smaller cities. In Tulsa, Oklahoma, in 1921, over 300 African Americans died in race riots, and 1,200 were left homeless.

During race riots, a large part of Walnut Street in East St. Louis, Illinois, was burned down.

Problems in Britain

Racial problems also occurred in British cities. Fighting broke out in London and Liverpool in 1919. More trouble started in Cardiff. Thousands of African men had been enlisted from Britain's **colonies** in Africa to serve in World War I. Others were hired from the colonies to work in Britain in jobs left behind by British soldiers fighting at the Front.

When the war ended in 1919, many returning soldiers wanted the Africans immediately returned to Africa. British whites said the new arrivals had no right to jobs in Britain. Rioting broke out during the summer of 1919. Some factory owners were forced to fire all their African workers. The African men fought back when attacked. Many were imprisoned.

World War I finally ended in November 1918. British troops marched in victory through the streets of London on 19 July 1919.

The Pan-African movement

At the dawn of the 1900s, many blacks were looking for ways to fight the oppression and racism that had existed since the early days of slavery. Some worked to unite blacks everywhere for a common cause they called **Pan-Africanism**. In 1900 the first Pan-African conference was held in London to address the needs of people of African origin. It protested the unequal treatment of blacks in British colonies and called for better treatment of blacks worldwide. Speakers also pointed out the many achievements of blacks around the world. The conference was the beginning of a movement that would last throughout the century, including several more conferences.

The Pan-African Congress of 1921 produced a bold statement called the "London Manifesto". It proclaimed that Britain was still enslaving its black subjects. It claimed that blacks were not being trained in self-government, nor given rights allowed to white men. It demanded change.

This photograph shows a Pan-African Conference meeting in 1921.

The Universal Races Congress

In 1911 another worldwide meeting was held in London to fight racism. The Universal Races Congress brought together over 1,000 people from 50 countries to fight the idea that some races were smarter, stronger, or more advanced than others. One organizer concluded with the statement that people of all races were "essentially equal in intellect, enterprise, morality and physique".

Marcus Garvey

One leader in the Pan-African cause was Marcus Garvey. Born in Jamaica in 1887, Garvey became editor of several newspapers. He founded the Universal Negro Improvement Association (UNIA), whose ultimate goal was to unite people of African ancestry under one nation. Garvey started an American branch of his organization in Harlem, New York, and sent delegates to the Pan-African Congress of 1919. His newspaper *Negro World* was widely read.

Garvey wanted to redevelop Liberia in Africa as a homeland for blacks around the world. The government of Liberia did not agree to open their borders to "everyone" – only those who would contribute to the economy. American whites feared Garvey's drive for black power, and the government forced him to leave the country. When he died in 1940, millions of blacks supported his goals of racial pride and unity.

An artistic rebirth

After racial violence occurred in lower New York City, Philip Payton and his Afro-American Realty Company encouraged blacks to rent homes in the Harlem district, in the northern part of the city. Others moved to Harlem from the South, and families arrived from the Caribbean. Soon the neighbourhood was home to 175,000 black residents, and the sense of community grew.

Artists living in Harlem explored the experience of being African American in music, song, fine art, poetry, and prose. In 1925 the national magazine *The Survey Graphic* devoted an issue to the culture developing in Harlem. The following year a popular novel described the neighbourhood to the world. This brought more people into Harlem, including writers, artists, and musicians. Together the residents of Harlem created a revival of arts and culture. It became known as the **Harlem Renaissance**.

The Cotton Club in Harlem, New York, featured the best black performers – for all-white audiences.

Author Langston Hughes was one of the most influential writers of the Harlem Renaissance.

New African-American voices emerge

Two of the most important writers from the Harlem Renaissance were Langston Hughes and Zora Neale Hurston. Hughes was born in 1902. After attending university in Pennsylvania, he moved to Harlem, where he wrote novels, poems, and essays. Hughes's writings captured the emotions and the rhythms of Harlem life and encouraged racial pride. He talked about the new "Negro identity", saying, "We younger Negro artists now intend to express our individual dark-skinned selves without fear or shame. If white people are pleased we are glad. If they aren't, it doesn't matter. We know we are beautiful."

Zora Neale Hurston was born in 1891. A talented student, Hurston graduated from Columbia University in New York. She settled in Harlem to write stories, novels, and collect folklore about African Americans and Caribbean blacks. She explored the African roots of African-American culture. In 1926 Hurston edited a literary magazine called *Fire!!* with Langston Hughes. They showcased other Harlem writers. Her novel, *Their Eyes Were Watching God*, caused controversy. It discussed divisions between blacks with lighter and darker skins. The characters in it used simple black **dialect**. This portrait of the black community made some uncomfortable.

Black Caribbean writers emerge

Black people in the Caribbean **colonies** were impatient with continuing inequality. On all the islands, black residents were in the large majority. But none had elected representatives. All governing came from their colonial ruler.

Some people reacted to this treatment with violence. In 1903, for example, blacks from the British-ruled island of Trinidad **rioted** over British attempts to impose taxes on water. They burned the seat of government down. Others expressed their frustration through writing. A new group of writers emerged who would share with the world the experience of blacks from the Caribbean.

The Trinidad awakening

C. L. R. James, Ralph Mentor, and Alfred Mendes were black men from Trinidad. They wrote fiction, poetry, and essays in magazines like *The Beacon* and *Trinidad Magazine* in the 1930s. They explored the clash of white and black cultures in the Caribbean through their characters and situations. They looked at the poverty and **discrimination** against the black community. With others, they formed what was called the "Trinidad Awakening" in literature.

Négritude

In the 1930s, a new black literary and political movement rose up around the world called Négritude, which is French for "blackness". The movement's leaders, who were mostly French-speaking blacks, believed that blacks should celebrate their race and history. The movement also spoke out against European treatment of blacks, especially the period of colonisation.

The Négritude movement was influenced by Harlem Renaissance writers such as Langston Hughes and Richard Wright. Among its followers were Aimé Césaire, a poet from Martinique, and Léopold Sédar Senghor, who later became the president of Senegal in Africa. Césaire defined Négritude as "the simple recognition that one is black, the acceptance of this fact and our destiny as blacks, of our history and culture".

Afro-Cuban writers

Marcelino Arozarena and Nicolas Guillen were Afro-Cuban poets and journalists. They founded the *poesia negra* (black poetry) movement in Cuba after the country gained independence. Both men were strongly influenced by African music, rhythms, and rhymes. They used African folklore descriptions and themes. They combined all these to create exciting new black poetry.

Claude McKay

Claude McKay was born in Jamaica in 1889. He created poetry about his homeland. Then he moved to Harlem in New York and became a writer of the Harlem Renaissance. McKay decried racism in his poetry. His novel *Home to Harlem* (1928) was the first American bestseller by a black writer. It attracted both white and black readers.

Black musical traditions

In New Orleans, USA, in the 1800s, slaves were allowed to gather in Congo Square on Sundays. Here they performed traditional African music and dances. They formed a circle, often gathering with members of the same African tribe, and played drums and whatever other instruments were available.

Although the gatherings in Congo Square ended before the Civil War, enslaved Africans built on their musical traditions. Slavery brought on a new musical style. To pass time as they worked, often one enslaved African would call out a line, and others would repeat it back. Then everyone would call out a new line. This "call and response" style, combined with traditional African music and other music of the time, would evolve into new forms, including ragtime, blues, and jazz.

Ragtime music

Ragtime music developed in the 1890s. This music fused African-American style with European band music and instruments such as strings and woodwinds. Ragtime was dance music created by black composers for black audiences. Soon white listeners wanted to dance along to this bouncy beat. Leading ragtime composer Scott Joplin published his "Original Rags" in 1899.

This illustration shows African Americans dancing and singing in New Orleans in the 1800s.

The blues

Blues music grew out of the "call and response" field songs of slavery, as well as African and American musical traditions. The instruments used were mainly guitar, harmonica, drums, and later a piano. These songs told stories of passion, love affairs, and loneliness. Blues music had a strong influence on later styles such as rock and roll.

Robert Johnson

Robert Johnson was virtually unknown during his life, but his few recordings influenced the careers of blues and rock musicians such as Muddy Waters, Led Zeppelin, Eric Clapton, and Bob Dylan.

Johnson was born in 1911 in Mississippi, USA and grew up outside Memphis. He loved to sing blues songs and played them on his harmonica. He got his guitar training in "jook" houses (African-American bars with music). During hard times in the 1930s, Johnson wrote songs blending African and European legends, such as the symbol of the crossroads in life, Christian beliefs about the soul and the devil, and deep African-American spiritual traditions. In his song "Rambling on my Mind", he sang about his belief that his life would be short. Johnson died of poisoning at age 27.

Jazz

Jazz was another form of music that evolved from the blues. More instruments were added, and melodies were complex. Jazz musicians began to **improvise**, or play sections of music they made up on the spot. Great jazz performers included Louis Armstrong, Duke Ellington, and Ferdinand "Jelly Roll" Morton.

Music around the world

The influence of black culture was felt in musical forms all over the world. In Central and South America, African influences led to a festive new form of music and dance known as salsa. The samba is danced in Brazil and comes from African and European roots. Black musicians such as Samuel Coleridge-Taylor in Britain influenced the world of classical music, while African-American singer and dancer Josephine Baker made her mark on the stage in Paris.

Edward "Duke" Ellington

An American pianist, composer and bandleader, Ellington was born in Washington, D.C., in 1899. By 1923 he had moved to Harlem, New York. He composed and arranged music, and played for the stage, the nightclub, and the ballroom. He adapted ragtime and the blues, blending his own melodies and styles. Both white and black music lovers embraced his innovative style.

Samuel Coleridge-Taylor

Samuel Coleridge-Taylor was born in England in 1875 to a white British mother and a father from Sierra Leone. Coleridge-Taylor was a brilliant violinist and composer. He was the first black composer to use African rhythms in classical compositions. He wrote music to the poetry of Paul Lawrence Dunbar, an African-American author. Dunbar, the son of a slave, lived from 1872 to 1906. In his short life, Dunbar published twelve books of poetry, four books of short stories, five novels, and a play.

Coleridge-Taylor gained fame for composing music to Henry Wadsworth Longfellow's epic poem "Song of Hiawatha". He also loved the music of American spirituals and set "24 Negro Melodies" to symphonic music.

British musician Samuel Coleridge-Taylor (1875–1912) gained fame for composing classical music to poetry.

Josephine Baker

Born in St. Louis, USA, in 1906, Baker was a black singer, dancer, and comic. New York theatre producers cast her in *Shuffle Along*, Broadway's first hit black musical, in 1921. But she could not win leading roles with whites. So in the 1920s, Baker moved to Paris, France. There she became the darling of the French theatre. By 1927 she was earning more money than any other stage performer in Europe. Baker believed in unity between all races. She adopted 12 mixed-race children from around the world.

Blacks take centre stage

Blacks had to struggle to be recognized as top actors, artists, and athletes. Throughout the 1800s, there were few chances for black actors to be trained or play leading roles. Most actors had to play servant roles in white companies. Yet some had the drive and talent to get the top roles. Two pioneer theatre performers were Ira Aldridge and Paul Robeson.

Ira Aldridge

Born in 1807 in New York City, Aldridge attended the Afro-American Free School and longed to become an actor. An African-American theatre troupe, the African Grove Theatre, cast him in roles. But directors were afraid that

audiences would not accept an African-American leading man in a white company. So Aldridge tried the London stage, but some biased critics were unhappy to see him working with white actresses in Shakespeare's plays. He toured the country, developing his skills, and then played leading roles in Shakespearean plays in the best theatres in Germany, Austria, Poland, and Russia.

Ira Aldridge (1807–67) was one of the first black actors to play leading roles in Shakespeare's plays.

Paul Robeson

Robeson, an African-American actor and singer, found success as a performer in the 1920s and 1930s. Raised in New Jersey, USA, he was a top student at university and played professional American football. In 1921 he got his singing break in a Broadway show called *Shuffle Along*, alongside Josephine Baker. In 1924 and 1925, Robeson starred in two Eugene O'Neill plays, becoming the first African-American actor to star in a white Broadway company. Robeson also starred in other shows, films, and concerts, and sang on records both in Britain and the United States.

Later, Robeson became disgusted with racial prejudice in the United States. He joined the **Communist Party** in protest. This unpopular move kept him from working for many years. Robeson taught himself many languages. This allowed him to tour the world and seek justice for all races.

Black athletes

Black athletes hoping to succeed on the biggest stages had to do more than defeat their opponents. They also had to combat **prejudice** and hatred. These athletes did not earn the prestige or money their white counterparts earned. Athletes in some sports were able to compete alongside whites, but many faced racism when they did.

Football

One of the first black British footballers was Walter Tull, who was born in 1888. Both his parents died by the time he was nine, and he went to live in an orphanage. He played football for the orphanage team, and later became a star on both amateur and professional teams, despite facing racism.

Tull's football career ended in 1914, when he went to fight in World War I. A strong leader, Tull was promoted to sergeant. After returning home to recover from illness, he was trained as an officer, despite rules that forbade blacks from becoming officers. He led British troops in Italy and Germany as the first black British officer. After being killed in battle in 1918, Tull was awarded the British War and Victory Medal.

Baseball

In the United States, black baseball players were **segregated** into the Negro League, where they were poorly paid and received little recognition. Players such as Josh Gibson, who may have hit more home runs than anyone in baseball history, are not well known today.

Walter Tull (1888–1918), one of the first black British footballers, died fighting in World War I.

Tennis

Lucy Diggs Slowe was the first African-American woman ever to win a national tennis title. She won the American Tennis Association's tournament in 1917. This was just one of Slowe's many firsts. In university she helped to found the first **sorority** for African-American women. Later she became the first Dean of Women at Howard University in Washington, D.C., where she created a women's campus. She helped to organize the National Association of College Women, which helped raise women's standing at US universities.

Jesse Owens and the 1936 Olympics

The 1936 Olympic Games were hosted by Germany. The country's leader at the time was Adolf Hitler, head of the **Nazi** party. Hitler believed that whites were smarter, stronger, and better than people of any other race. Hitler hoped that the Olympics would prove him right.

But African-American track and field competitor Jesse Owens didn't let that happen. Owens captured four gold medals. In all, African-American athletes won 14 of the United States' 56 medals at the Olympics that year.

Jesse Owens races towards a gold medal in the 1936 Olympic games.

Black artists

In the early 1900s, many talented black artists emerged, though many went unrecognized. Two of these were William H. Johnson and Jacob Lawrence.

William H. Johnson was born in 1901 in South Carolina, USA. One of the first successful African-American artists, Johnson struggled to receive an art education in New York. Through grants and awards, he travelled to Paris in 1926, where he studied and painted. His marriage to a white woman was unacceptable in the United States, so Johnson remained in Europe. His paintings included many scenes of African-American family life. His true recognition did not come until after his death in 1970.

Jacob Lawrence was born in 1917 and educated in Harlem, New York. He explored black historical subjects in his painting. In 1937 he painted a series on Haiti's slave rebellion. He also produced a series of works on abolitionist Frederick Douglass and on Harriet Tubman leading slaves to freedom. Other works showed blacks migrating to big cities. Lawrence's powerful images made black history come alive.

Jacob Lawrence painted *The Library* in 1960.

Progress made

From 1870 to the late 1930s, blacks around the world struggled to recover from the effects of slavery. In Britain and Europe, blacks faced **discrimination** and resentment. Blacks in the Americas faced a life with many obstacles: little money or education, a lack of government support, and often the hostility of whites. Africans were taking even longer to recover from the previous centuries, as the destructive slave trade was replaced with colonisation by European powers.

Despite these challenges, many blacks made their marks by asserting their freedom and expressing themselves. Great writers emerged. Some spoke forcefully about the rights of blacks, while others evoked unique images through poetry and novels. New, influential forms of music developed, from ragtime to blues and jazz. Blacks in all fields, from athletics to science, proved that they could meet or exceed the accomplishments of anyone. It would be a long time before they would be recognised as equals. But blacks around the world had established a legacy that they would build on for years to come.

Timeline

1865	The United States frees its slaves.
1866	The United States government sets up the Freedmen's Bureau.
1866	The **Ku Klux Klan** organizes in the United States.
1870	United States passes the 15th **Amendment**, giving all men the right to vote. Hiram Revels becomes first African American in the United States Senate.
1875	United States passes its Civil Rights Act to ban **discrimination** by race. Blanche K. Bruce is elected to the United States Senate.
1879	Zulu forces defeat the British in South Africa. Their victory is short-lived.
1881	Booker T. Washington founds the Tuskegee Institute.
1882	Andrew Watson is the first black footballer in Scotland.
1883	The United States **Supreme Court** strikes down the Civil Rights Act.
1884	Berlin Conference in Germany divides Africa between European powers. Britain, France, Belgium, the Netherlands, Germany, and others conquer African territories.
1886	Cuba frees its slaves.
1888	Brazil frees its slaves.
1896	*Plessy v. Ferguson* case decided in United States Supreme Court, upholding "separate but equal" situation for blacks.
1897	"Harlem Rag", the first black instrumental rag, is published in New York.
1898	Cuba wins independence from Spain.
1900	First Pan-African Conference is held in London, to work for African rights.
1900	Nigeria becomes a British Protectorate.

1906	First American race **riot** takes place in Atlanta, USA.
1908	Race riot takes place in Springfield, USA.
1909	The National Association for the Advancement of Colored People is formed.
1914	World War I begins in Europe.
1917	Race riot takes place in East St. Louis, Illinois.
1917	Lucy Diggs Slowe wins tennis championship, becoming first black woman to win a national sports title.
1918	First black British officer, Walter Tull, is killed in action.
1918	World War I ends.
1919	Race riots take place in London and Liverpool.
1921	"London Manifesto" is published by Pan-African Congress.
1921	First black-written musical opens on Broadway in New York.
1923	NAACP wins Supreme Court ruling allowing blacks to serve on juries.
1924	Paul Robeson becomes first black actor to star in two Broadway shows.
1927	African-American singer Josephine Baker becomes highest paid performer in Europe.
1936	United States Olympic team fields 18 black athletes, 10 of whom win medals. Track star Jesse Owens wins four gold medals.

Glossary

amendment addition to a document. Amendments to the United States Constitution gave new rights to people.

Black Codes laws passed in the United States in 1800s to limit the civil rights of African Americans

colony distant territory under the control of another nation

Communist Party political party that believes that property and goods should be held in common

constitution ideas according to which a country or state is governed

dialect manner of speaking

discrimination treating someone differently because of race

distillery place where alcohol is made

emancipation freeing or liberating of people from slavery

Harlem Renaissance African-American artistic movement that took place in Harlem, New York

immigrant person who moves to another place to live

improvise to create on the spot. Jazz music was often improvised.

indentured when a person is contracted to serve another for a certain period of time

intermarriage marriage between members of different races or groups

Jim Crow term for laws designed to keep blacks and whites separate

Ku Klux Klan organization started in the southern United States in 1866 to keep white people in power and frighten non-whites

lynching illegal execution by mob violence, usually because of the victim's race

manhood suffrage all adult males allowed to vote regardless of their race, religion, or income

migration movement of a group of people from one area to another

militant aggressive

National Guard military force for the defence of the United States

Nazi Party political party that controlled Germany from 1933 to 1945. Nazis believed in the supremacy of the white race.

Pan-Africanism term for the movement to unite all African nations

plantation large farm or estate that usually grows a single crop

prejudice dislike of people, sometimes only because of their race

protectorate territory protected by the British government

riot uncontrolled mob violence that damages property and usually injures or kills people

segregation keeping one group separate or apart from other groups

senate part of the United States governing body, similar to the House of Lords

sharecropping renting sections of another man's land for a share of the profit from the crop

sorority social group of women usually set up in college or university

Supreme Court the highest court of law in the United States

Western describes the western hemisphere of the world

Find out more

Books

American Lives: W.E.B. DuBois, Jennifer Blizen Gillis (Heinemann Library, 2006)

A History of American Music: Jazz and *Blues,* Christopher Handyside (Heinemann Library, 2006)

Ida B. Wells-Barnett: Strike a Blow Against a Glaring Evil, Anne E. Schraff (Enslow, 2008)

Websites

Biography of Walter Tull
http://www.100greatblackbritons.com/bios/walter_tull.html

Gallery of images from the life of Samuel Coleridge-Taylor
http://www.bl.uk/onlinegallery/features/blackeuro/coleridgebackground.html

Biographies and timeline of Harlem Renaissance
http://www.si/umich.edu/CHICO/Harlem/text/exhibition.html

Index